P9-CQZ-091

Weekly Reader Books presents

A Kid's TV Guide

A Children's Book about Watching TV Intelligently

by

Joy Wilt

Illustrated by Ernie Hergenroeder

Educational Products Division
Word, Incorporated
Waco, Texas

Author

JOY WILT is creator and director of Children's Ministries, an organization that provides resources "for people who care about children"—speakers, workshops, demonstrations, consulting services, and training institutes. A certified elementary school teacher, administrator, and early childhood specialist, Joy is also consultant to and professor in the master's degree program in children's ministries for Fuller Theological Seminary. Joy is a graduate of LaVerne College, LaVerne, California (B.A. in Biological Science), and Pacific Oaks College, Pasadena, California (M.A. in Human Development). She is author of three books, *Happily Ever After, An Uncomplicated Guide to Becoming a Superparent,* and *Taming the Big Bad Wolves,* as well as the popular *Can-Make-And-Do Books.* Joy's commitment "never to forget what it feels like to be a child" permeates the many innovative programs she has developed and her work as lecturer, consultant, writer, and—not least—mother of two children, Christopher and Lisa.

Artist

ERNIE HERGENROEDER is founder and owner of Hergie & Associates (a visual communications studio and advertising agency). With the establishment of this company in 1975, "Hergie" and his wife, Faith, settled in San Jose with their four children, Lynn, Kathy, Stephen, and Beth. Active in community and church affairs, Hergie is involved in presenting creative workshops for teachers, ministers, and others who wish to understand the techniques of communicating visually. He also lectures in high schools to encourage young artists toward a career in commercial art. Hergie serves as a consultant to organizations such as the Police Athletic League (PAL), Girl Scouts, and religious and secular corporations. His ultimate goal is to touch the hearts of kids (8 to 80) all over the world—visually!

This book is a presentation of Weekly Reader Books.
Weekly Reader Books offers book clubs for children from
preschool through junior high school.

For further information write to:
WEEKLY READER BOOKS
1250 Fairwood Ave.
Columbus, Ohio 43216

A Kid's TV Guide

Copyright © 1979 by Joy Wilt. All rights reserved. Printed in the United States of America. No part of this book may be used or reproduced in any manner whatsoever without written permission, except in the case of brief quotations embodied in critical articles and reviews.

This edition is published by arrangement with Educational Products Division, Word, Incorporated, 4800 West Waco Drive, Waco, Texas 76710.

ISBN: 0-8499-8133-6
Library of Congress Catalog Card Number: 79-50043
Bruce Johnson, Editor

6 7 8 9 / 86 85 84

Contents

Introduction

<u>A Kid's TV Guide</u> is one of a series of books. The complete set is called *Ready-Set-Grow!*

<u>A Kid's TV Guide</u> deals with watching television intelligently and can be used by itself or as a part of a program that utilizes all the the *Ready-Set-Grow!* books.

<u>A Kid's TV Guide</u> is specifically designed so that children can either read the book themselves or have it read to them. This can be done at home, church, or school. When reading to children, it is not necessary to complete the book at one sitting. Concern should be given to the attention span of the individual child and his or her comprehension of the subject matter.

<u>A Kid's TV Guide</u> is designed to involve the child in the concepts that are being taught. This is done by simply and carefully explaining each concept and then asking questions that invite a response from the child. It is hoped that by answering the questions, the child will personalize the concept and, thus, integrate it into his or her thinking.

<u>A Kid's TV Guide</u> teaches that watching television can be a very good thing—if it is done wisely and properly controlled. TV can be entertaining, educational, informative, thought provoking, and relaxing—or it can cause people to want things that are not good for them, escape from reality, be passive and uncreative, or even become violent.

A television cannot turn itself on or off; people do that. People are also capable of thinking about what they see on television, rather than passively accepting it

A Kid's TV Guide is designed to teach children how to watch television safely and wisely. It tells children how to keep their bodies safe, how to choose the programs they will watch, and how to evaluate tempting advertisements.

Recently there has been a great deal of public interest about the possible harm that television can do to children. But more American families have televisions than have indoor plumbing. As a form of readily available entertainment, television is very attractive to children. And it can be a powerful educational and persuasive tool. For these reasons, it is very important that children learn to control television—and not let it control them.

A Kid's TV Guide

No matter who you are, no matter where you live, chances are you watch TV.

This is because in almost every home there is at least one TV.

In fact, more Americans have television sets than indoor plumbing.

Your family probably owns a TV, and you probably began watching at a very early age.

By the time you graduate from high school, you will probably have spent 15,000 hours watching TV. This is more time than you will have spent doing anything else, except sleeping!

During the 15,000 hours you watch TV, you will see about 350,000 commercials.

You will also see about 18,000 murders.

What can all this watching TV do to you? Can it affect you in any way?

Some parents, doctors, teachers, and other concerned adults think that it can.

Chapter 1

Watching TV Can Be Harmful

TV can possibly influence you to want and buy things that are not good for you.

THAT LOOKS YUMMY. I'D SURE LIKE TO HAVE SOME!

SUGAR ROCKS

Too often TV can cause a person to run away from problems instead of facing them and trying to solve them.

Too often TV can take the place of spending time with friends and other people.

23

TV can possibly take the place of doing creative things.

25

TV can possibly cause you to become a "watcher" instead of a "doer."

Being a "watcher" is not good because you can't grow into a healthy human being by standing back and watching all the time. In order to learn and grow, it is important to become actively involved in the things that are happening around you.

28

TV can possibly cause you to become aggressive and perhaps even violent. 29

TV can possibly cause you to do things that are not good for you or for other people.

TV can make you think things about the world that aren't true.

NOW THAT'S THE WAY FAMILIES SHOULD BE. I'LL BET MOST FAMILIES ARE LIKE THAT. SOMEHOW I GOT STUCK WITH A WEIRD FAMILY.

If it is true that . . .

TV can possibly influence a person to want and buy things that are not good for him or her,

TV can cause a person to run away from problems instead of facing them and trying to solve them,

TV can possibly take the place of spending time with friends and other people,

TV can possibly take the place of doing creative things,

TV can possibly cause a person to become a "watcher" instead of a "doer,"

TV can possibly cause a person to become aggressive and perhaps even violent,

TV can possibly cause a person to do things that are not good for him or her or for other people, and

TV can make a person think things about the world that aren't true . . .

should anyone watch TV at all?

Should you completely stop watching TV?

Before you decide to stop watching TV altogether . . .

stop and think!

A television set is only an electrical appliance.

It cannot think.

It cannot turn itself on.

It cannot turn itself off.

But . . .

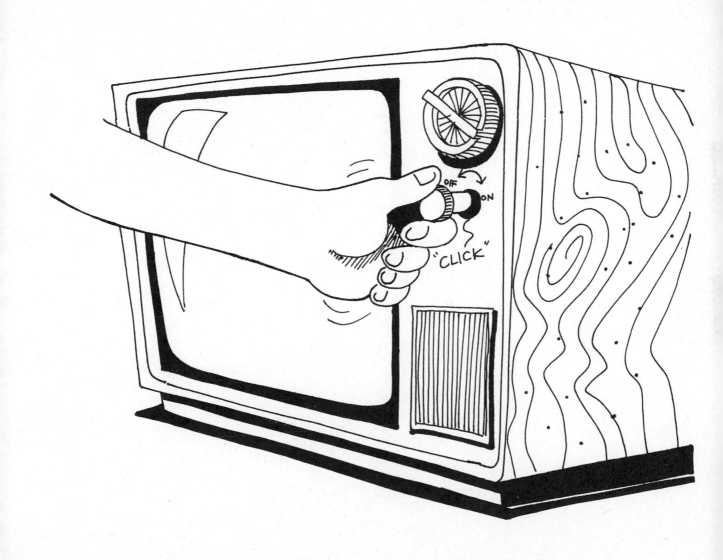

You can think.   You can turn a TV on.   You can turn a TV off.

You do not have to be controlled by TV. Instead, you can and should control TV.

TV cannot hurt you if you control it and use it wisely. **41**

A TV that is controlled properly and used wisely can be a very good thing.

Chapter 2

Watching TV Can Be Helpful

When used properly, TV can give you good entertainment.

TV can bring about interesting conversation between you and other people.

45

When used properly, TV can show you new ideas.

TV can broaden your view of the world.

47

When used properly, TV can teach you educational facts and information.

When used properly, TV can help you relax and unwind. **49**

So, TV can be a good thing.

TV can give you good entertainment.

TV can bring about interesting conversation between you and other people.

TV can show you new ideas.

TV can broaden your view of the world.

TV can teach you educational facts and information.

TV can help you relax and unwind.

But if watching TV is to be helpful instead of harmful, you need to . . .

watch TV moderately,

watch TV safely,

choose the right TV programs to watch, and

watch TV commercials critically.

Chapter 3

Watching TV Moderately

Food is a good thing.

But eating too much food is not good for you.

Exercise is a good thing.

But too much exercise at one time is not good for you.

It has been said that too much of anything is not good for a person.

And so it is with TV.

THIS ENDS ANOTHER DAY OF BROADCAST ON WREC-TV. GOOD NIGHT!

TV can be a good thing, but watching too much TV can be harmful.   59

So how much TV is too much?
Some experts say . . .

Other experts say . . .

But experts can only make suggestions. It is up to you and your parents to decide whether you will watch TV for

1 hour,

2 hours,

3 hours, or

4 hours every day.

Whatever you and your parents decide, both of you need to know and remember that . . .

you should not watch more than four hours of TV a day, and

it is not good for you to watch TV for more than two hours at a time.

Watching TV can be a good thing if you watch moderately.

Chapter 4

Watching TV Safely

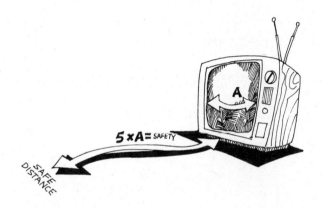

Many doctors have warned . . .

TV Rule #1

<u>Do not sit too close to the TV set while watching.</u>

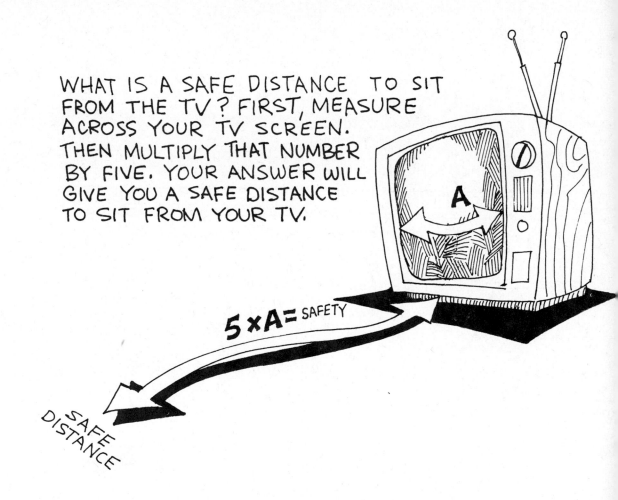

WHAT IS A SAFE DISTANCE TO SIT FROM THE TV? FIRST, MEASURE ACROSS YOUR TV SCREEN. THEN MULTIPLY THAT NUMBER BY FIVE. YOUR ANSWER WILL GIVE YOU A SAFE DISTANCE TO SIT FROM YOUR TV.

$5 \times A = $ SAFETY

SAFE DISTANCE

TV Rule #2

Do not wear sunglasses while you watch TV.

TV Rule #3

<u>Do not watch TV in a completely dark room.</u>

TV Rule #4

Do not put the TV where you will see glare or reflections from lights or windows.

TV Rule #5

<u>While watching TV do not turn the sound above a normal listening level.</u>

TV Rule #6

Remember that a TV is an electrical appliance that must be handled with extreme caution.

ZAP

YOU WILL DO YOURSELF A FAVOR BY FOLLOWING ALL SIX OF THESE SIMPLE RULES.

1. DO NOT SIT TOO CLOSE TO YOUR TV SET.
2. DO NOT WEAR SUNGLASSES WHILE WATCHING TV.
3. DO NOT WATCH YOUR TV IN A COMPLETELY DARK ROOM.
4. PLACE TV AWAY FROM LIGHTS OR WINDOWS TO PREVENT GLARE.
5. KEEP THE SOUND AT A NORMAL LISTENING LEVEL.
6. HANDLE WITH EXTREME CAUTION.

Chapter 5

Choosing the Right Programs to Watch on TV

Some TV programs are good for you to watch while others are not.

You and your parents can decide which programs are good and which are bad by asking yourselves certain questions.

Question #1

Is the program interesting and entertaining?

Question #2

Is the program something that I can understand?

Question #3

Will the program make me want to do healthy, worthwhile activities instead of harmful, destructive ones?

Question #4

Will the program teach worthwhile ideals, values, and beliefs? Is there a clear difference between right and wrong?

Question #5

Will the program help me appreciate and
understand myself and the world around
me?

Question #6

Does the program show uncertain endings to crime and violence? If there is crime, it should be overcome with law and order. If there is violence, it should not be shown as a way to solve problems.

Question #7

Will the program frighten or upset me in any way?

Question #8

Does the program make it clear what is real and what is not real?

These eight questions are not easy ones to answer.

Your parents may need to help you answer them.

This should be done before you watch a program.

Perhaps once a week or every day you and your parents could look through a TV Guide together. Using the eight questions as a guideline, decide what programs would be good for you to watch.

Once again, here are the questions that should be answered as you decide which TV programs you are going to watch.

#1   Is the program interesting and entertaining?

#2   Is the program something that I can understand?

#3   Will the program make me want to do healthy, worthwhile activities instead of harmful, destructive ones?

#4   Will the program teach worthwhile ideals, values, and beliefs? Is there a clear difference between right and wrong?

#5   Will the program help me appreciate and understand
      myself and the world around me?

#6   Does the program show uncertain endings to crime and
      violence?

#7   Will the program frighten or upset me in any way?

#8   Does the program make it clear what is real and what
      is not real?

If TV is to help you instead of harm you, you must choose the right TV programs to watch.

When there are no good programs to watch, it would be best to leave the TV off.

Chapter 6

Watching TV Commercials Critically

It takes a lot of people to make a TV program. There are the people you see on TV. There are the people who make cartoons.

Other people write scripts. Then there are the people who do all the technical work like running the TV cameras, lights, and sound.

All of these people need to be paid for their work. Money is also needed to rent or buy a TV studio and all of the costumes, sets, props, and equipment that are used to make a program.

Where does the money come from to make a TV program? Advertisers.

Advertisers are people who have a product they want to sell.

109

Advertisers "sponsor" TV programs. This means that they pay to have programs made and shown on TV.

It costs the advertisers a lot of money to do this, but it's worth it to them, because it gives them a chance to sell their products.

Here's how it works.

The advertisers (they are also called sponsors) show a TV program they hope people will want to see. While the people are watching, the sponsors break into the program and tell about their product.

It goes something like this . . .

1.

WOW! THAT SOUNDS LIKE A GREAT PROGRAM. I THINK I'LL WATCH IT.

AND NOW, TERRIFIC TOYS IS PROUD TO BRING YOU "I CAPTURED A GREAT WHITE SHARK WITH MY BARE HANDS." BUT BEFORE OUR SHOW BEGINS, HERE'S AN IMPORTANT MESSAGE.

2.

I'D BETTER NOT LEAVE THE TV. I DON'T WANT TO MISS THE FIRST OF THE MOVIE.

IF YOU DON'T HAVE TERRIFIC TOYS, YOU DON'T HAVE ANY TOYS AT ALL.

3.

4.

HMMM — THOSE TOYS LOOK PRETTY GOOD.

I WONDER IF THE SHARK CAGE WILL WORK?

WE INTERRUPT THIS PROGRAM TO BRING YOU THIS BRIEF MESSAGE ABOUT TERRIFIC TOYS.

5.

I'D BETTER NOT LEAVE THE TV NOW. I DON'T WANT TO MISS ANY OF THE MOVIE.

TERRIFIC TOYS ARE THE ONLY TOYS THAT ARE ANY FUN.

6.

I LIKE TERRIFIC TOYS.

THIS PROGRAM WAS BROUGHT TO YOU BY TERRIFIC TOYS.

7.

WOW! THAT WAS A GREAT MOVIE!

8.

I'VE JUST GOT TO HAVE A TERRIFIC TOY. I'M GOING TO ASK MOM FOR ONE RIGHT NOW.

By sponsoring a TV program, advertisers are able to get the attention of thousands of people. While the people are watching, the advertisers show commercials.

A commercial is an announcement that is made to talk someone into buying something.

There are some commercials made especially for you. They usually try to talk you into buying food, drinks, candy, games, and toys. Even though you may not be able to buy the product yourself, the advertisers hope that you will talk your parents into buying it for you.

Unfortunately, many people often believe everything they see and hear. This is how you can be easily tricked by TV commercials into buying things you shouldn't buy.

All too often, you might be talked into buying things that are not good for you to eat or safe for you to have.

In many ways, commercials can lead you into believing things that are not true. By using special sound effects, music, lighting, and photography, commercials can make things appear to be better than they really are.

COSMIC MAN IS ANOTHER GREAT TERRIFIC TOY!

CRASH

MY COSMIC MAN DOESN'T LOOK AS TERRIFIC AS THE ONE ON TV.

EVERY GIRL IN THE WORLD WANTS A TERRIFIC TERRI DOLL.
TERRIFIC TERRI DOLLS ARE FOR TERRIFIC KIDS. YOU
CAN'T BE TERRIFIC WITHOUT A TERRIFIC TOY.

I DON'T WANT TO BE LEFT OUT.
MAYBE I NEED TO GET A TERRIFIC
TERRI DOLL.

By saying certain things, commercials can make you
believe things that are not necessarily true.

119

Well, what should you do? Should you stop watching TV in order to avoid seeing commercials?

But if you are going to watch TV, if you are going to see commercials, you need to think. You need to be critical of what you see.

You should never buy anything that is advertised on TV without finding out all you can about it.

HERE IS ONE OF THOSE TOYS THAT WAS ADVERTISED ON TV. I WONDER IF IT IS AS GOOD AS THE COMMERCIAL SAID IT WAS.

You need to get more information on a product than the commercial gives you before you buy it.

Here are some good questions to ask before you buy a toy or game that is advertised on TV.

1. Can I use the item in more than one way? Will it stimulate my thinking, creativity, or physical activity?

2. How long will the item last? Is it strong enough to take normal wear when it is used?

3. Will the item work? Will it do what it is supposed to do?

4. Can I use the item on my own, or will I need a lot of help from an adult?

5. Is the item attractive to me? Is it something I would really want?

6. Is the item safe? Does it have sharp points or edges, pinch places like springs or hinges, or small parts that could be swallowed by a younger child? I should also make sure it can be cleaned, will not burn easily, won't cause allergies, or isn't poisonous.

Using these questions as guidelines, you can decide whether a game or toy is good for you to have.

Before buying any food or drink that is advertised on TV, you or your parents need to read the label on the product to find out whether it contains something that may be harmful to you.

WOW! LOOK AT HOW MUCH SUGAR THEY PUT IN THIS CEREAL. I DON'T THINK THAT MUCH SUGAR IS GOOD FOR YOU.

GOLLY, THEY NEVER SAID ANYTHING ABOUT ALL THAT SUGAR IN THE COMMERCIAL.

Parents can help you decide whether a product is good for you to put into your body.

Conclusion

* WATCH TV MODERATELY.
* WATCH TV SAFELY.
* CHOOSE THE RIGHT PROGRAMS TO WATCH.
* WATCH TV COMMERCIALS CRITICALLY.

TV, like anything else, can be good or bad for you. It all depends on how you use it.

To make sure TV has a good effect on you, remember to . . .

* WATCH TV MODERATELY.

* WATCH TV SAFELY.

* CHOOSE THE RIGHT PROGRAMS TO WATCH.

* WATCH TV COMMERCIALS CRITICALLY.

If you do these things . . .

TV can and will be a positive experience in your life.